THE
BIG
TIME

ROBERT
PATTINSON

VALERIE BODDEN

CREATIVE EDUCATION

ROBERT PATTINSON

TABLE OF CONTENTS

MEET ROBERT

Robert walks down a red carpet outside a theater. Fans scream his name. They hold out pieces of paper. Robert smiles and signs *autographs*. Then he goes inside to watch his new movie. Fans can't wait to see it!

Robert Pattinson is an actor. Fans around the world know him best for his part in the *Twilight* movies. Many people think he is one of the best young actors today.

Robert dresses up to attend the first showings of his movies

ROBERT'S CHILDHOOD

Robert was born May 13, 1986, in London, England. He lived with his parents and two older sisters. His sisters liked to tease him. Sometimes they made him dress like a girl.

Robert's sisters are named Elisabeth and Victoria

LONDON, ENGLAND

GETTING INTO ACTING

Robert began to act in school plays when he was six. But he did not plan to become an actor. He thought he would like to be a singer.

Robert (center) went to an all-boys school called Tower House

When he was 13, Robert started going to a school with a good acting program. Later, he starred in many ***community theater*** plays, too. When Robert was 17, he was in a television movie called *Ring of the Nibelungs*.

....

Robert became a big star four years after his first TV movie

THE BIG TIME

In 2005, Robert played the part of Cedric Diggory in *Harry Potter and the Goblet of Fire*. The movie was a hit. Soon Robert landed an even bigger role. He starred as the vampire Edward in the five *Twilight* movies.

Robert as a vampire (opposite) and as Cedric Diggory (right)

After *Twilight*, Robert was **cast** in many more movies, such as *Water for Elephants* and *Cosmopolis*. Robert has won many MTV Movie Awards and Teen Choice Awards. In 2008, Robert won the New Hollywood Award at the Hollywood Film Festival.

Robert starred with Reese Witherspoon in Water for Elephants

OFF THE SCREEN

When he is not acting, Robert likes to sing and play piano and guitar. Two of Robert's songs are in the first *Twilight* movie. Robert also likes to read, play with his dog, and spend time with his friends.

Robert lives in Los Angeles but likes going home to England, too

WHAT IS NEXT?

Robert planned to star in many more movies. He also hoped to write and *produce* his own films. Robert's movies are likely to draw fans to theaters for a long time to come!

Robert with Twilight *costars Kristen Stewart and Taylor Lautner*

WHAT ROBERT SAYS ABOUT ...

BEING FAMOUS

"I can't see any advantage to fame.... I've got the same 2 friends I've had since I was 12, and I can't see that changing."

DOING WHAT YOU LOVE

"Don't go into acting or music because you want to make money—just do it for the love of it."

HARRY POTTER

"I credit *Harry Potter* with everything else that's come since for me."

GLOSSARY

autographs signatures (in which a person signs his or her own name) of a famous person

cast chosen to be in a movie or play

community theater a group of people from a town or city who join together to put on plays

produce to take charge of and pay for the making of a movie

READ MORE

Hibbert, Clare. *Movie Star*. Mankato, Minn.: Sea-to-Sea, 2012.

Johnson, Robin. *Robert Pattinson*. New York: Crabtree, 2011.

WEBSITES

Robert Pattinson
http://Robertpattinson.org/
This is a website all about Robert, with lots of pictures.

Robert Pattinson Biography
http://www.people.com/people/Robert_pattinson/
This site has information about Robert's life and many pictures, too.

INDEX

PUBLISHED BY Creative Education
P.O. Box 227, Mankato, Minnesota 56002
Creative Education is an imprint of The Creative Company
www.thecreativecompany.us

DESIGN AND PRODUCTION BY Christine Vanderbeek
ART DIRECTION BY Rita Marshall
PRINTED IN the United States of America

PHOTOGRAPHS BY Alamy (AF archive), Corbis (Asadorian-Mejia/Splash/Splash News, Jackson Lee/Splash News, Stephane Reix/For Picture, Angelika Warmuth/dpa), Getty Images (Venturelli/WireImage), iStockphoto (Cole Vineyard), Newscom (3 ARTS ENTERTAINMENT/Album, WARNER BROS./CLOSE, MURRAY/Album, Whitehotpix/ZUMAPRESS), Shutterstock (Globe Turner, Jaguar PS, Northfoto, Joe Seer, vipflash, Debby Wong)

LIBRARY OF CONGRESS CATALOGING-IN-PUBLICATION DATA
Bodden, Valerie.
Robert Pattinson / Valerie Bodden.
p. cm. — (The big time)
Includes index.
Summary: An elementary introduction to the life, work, and popularity of Robert Pattinson, a British actor known for his roles in such hit movies as *Harry Potter and the Goblet of Fire* and *Twilight*.

ISBN 978-1-60818-478-1
1. Pattinson, Robert, 1986– —Juvenile literature. 2. Motion picture actors and actresses—Great Britain— Biography—Juvenile literature. 3. Singers—Great Britain—Biography—Juvenile literature. I. Title.
PN2598.P36.B63 2013
791.4302'8092—dc23 [B]   2013014263

FIRST EDITION
9 8 7 6 5 4 3 2 1